The Boy Who Dreamed

"He Could Fly"

Copyright 2015©

All rights reserved. No portion of this book may be reproduced, stored in a retrievable system, or transmitted in any form or by any means-electronic, mechanical, photocopy, recording, scanning, or other (except for brief quotations in critical reviews or articles) without the prior written permission of the publisher.

www.PoetryPete.com

www.Facebook.com/Poetrypete

Published by Poetry Pete Publishing ©

Library of Congress control number is on file

To Parents and Young Ones-
Hi, I'm Poetry Pete!
And here's a word to the wise:
Knowledge is power - or so it's been said,
but how do you get that information into your head?
Well, remember learning - learning is the key.
And if you love knowledge, it can set you free.
Yes, it can take you to places - you've never known -
so keep searching for it, because you're not alone.
Yes, this ... this is your moment - what will you do?
Always remember your dreams are up to you!

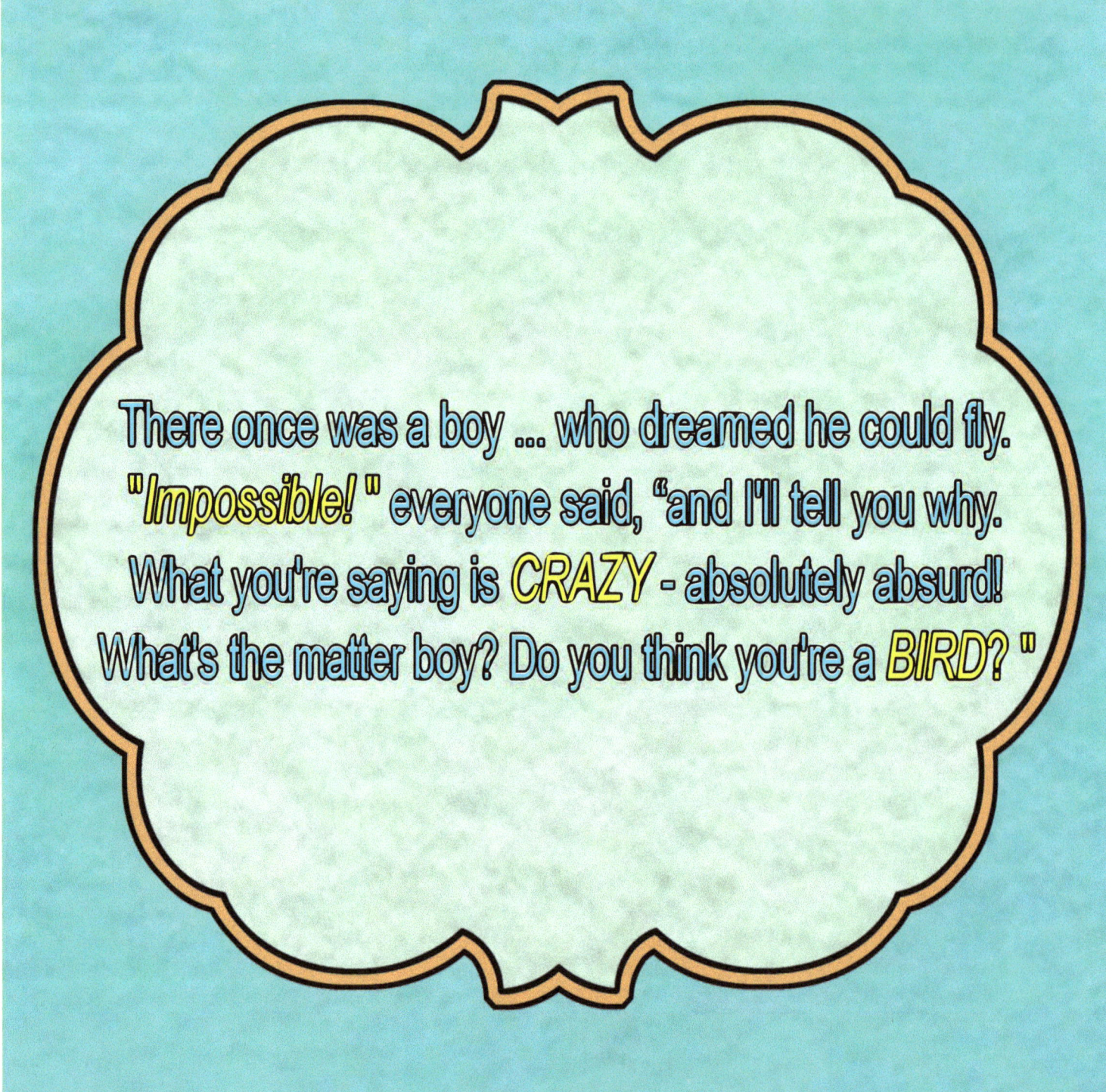

But he would say, "I'm NOT crazy, and I'm no fool!
I know what I'm saying, but I'll need to go to *school.*"

He'd think to himself, I may not be a bird or even a man, but if I put my mind to it and work at it, *I know I can*.

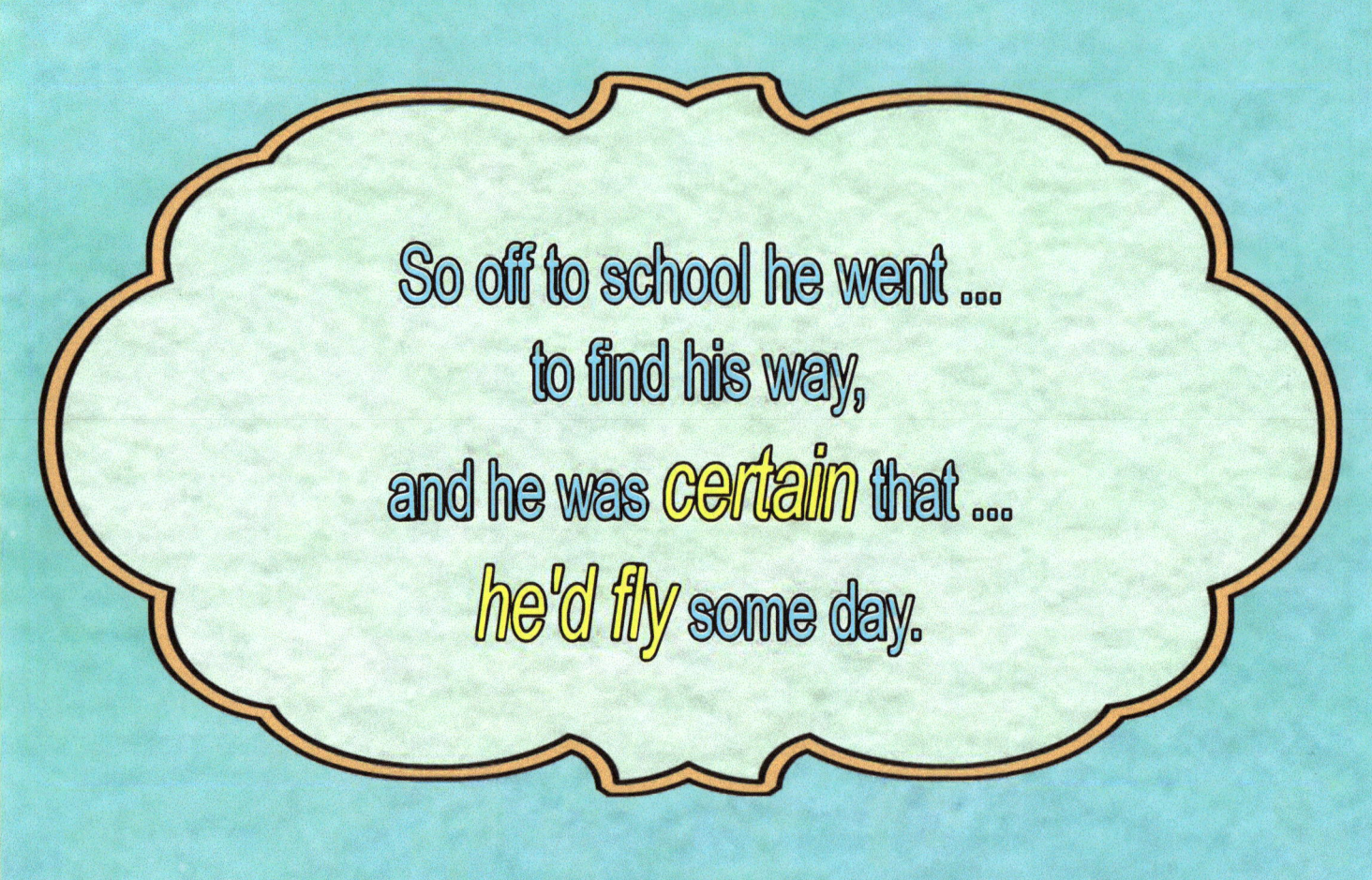

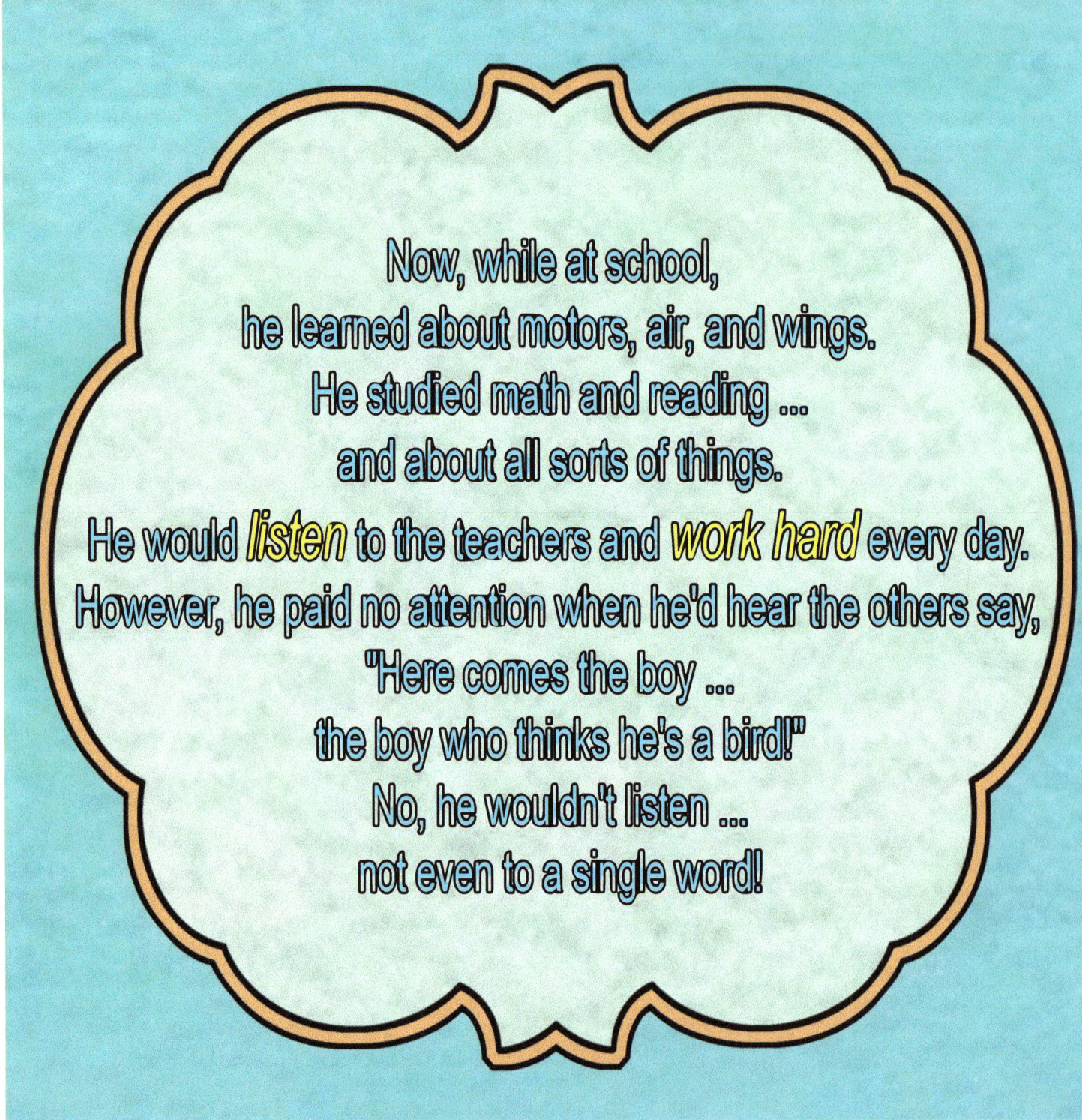

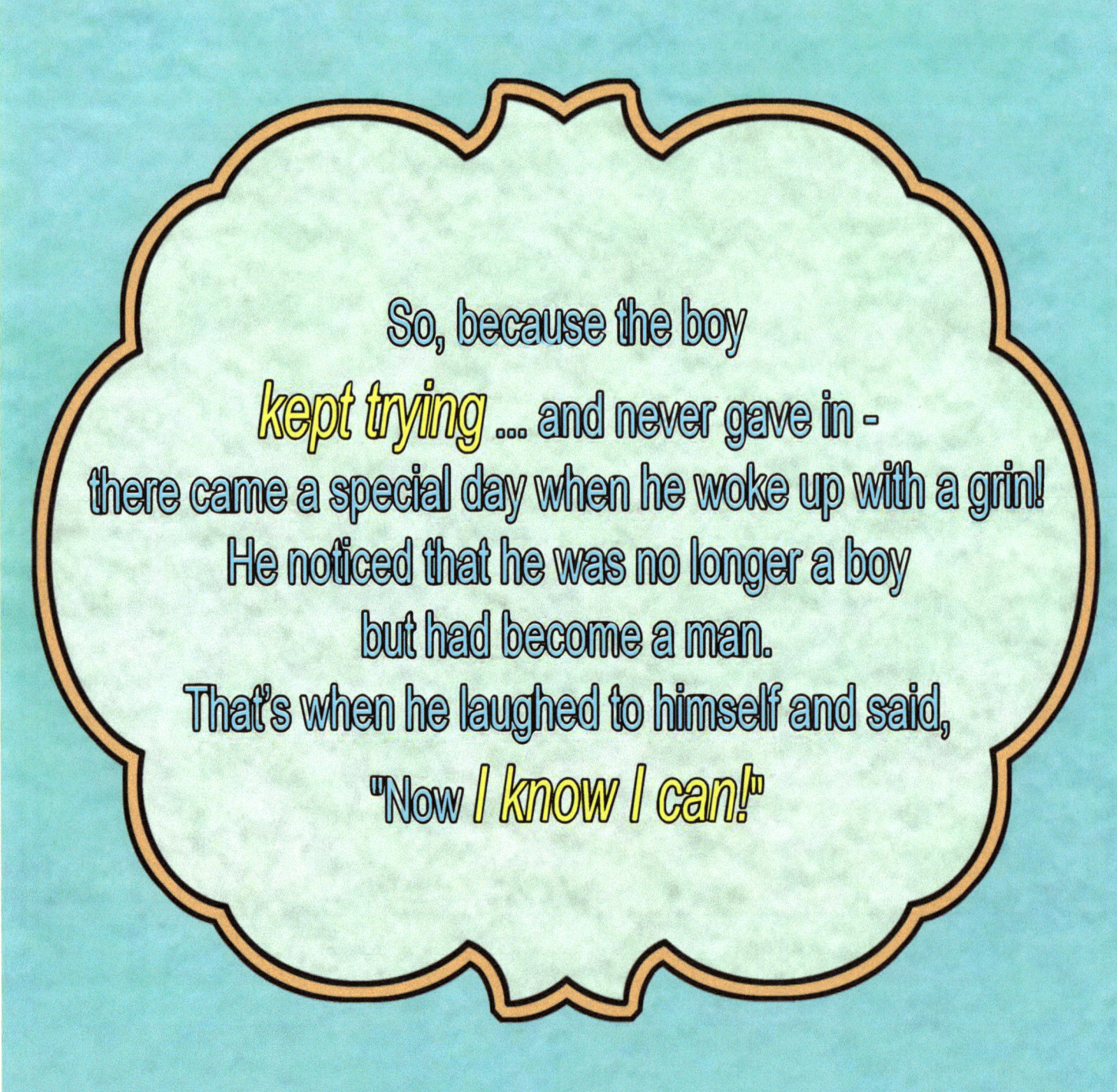

So, right away he said,
"I'll need something that can spin."
Then he thought to himself as he
smiled his special grin.
He said, "I'll need an engine - one that is really fast -
one that runs on jet fuel ... and one that will last!
I'll need wings that are, oh say, 20 feet long -
ones that won't give out, ones that are very strong.
I'll need a steering device to control which way I go."
Then he said to himself ...
the answer's simple -
I know!

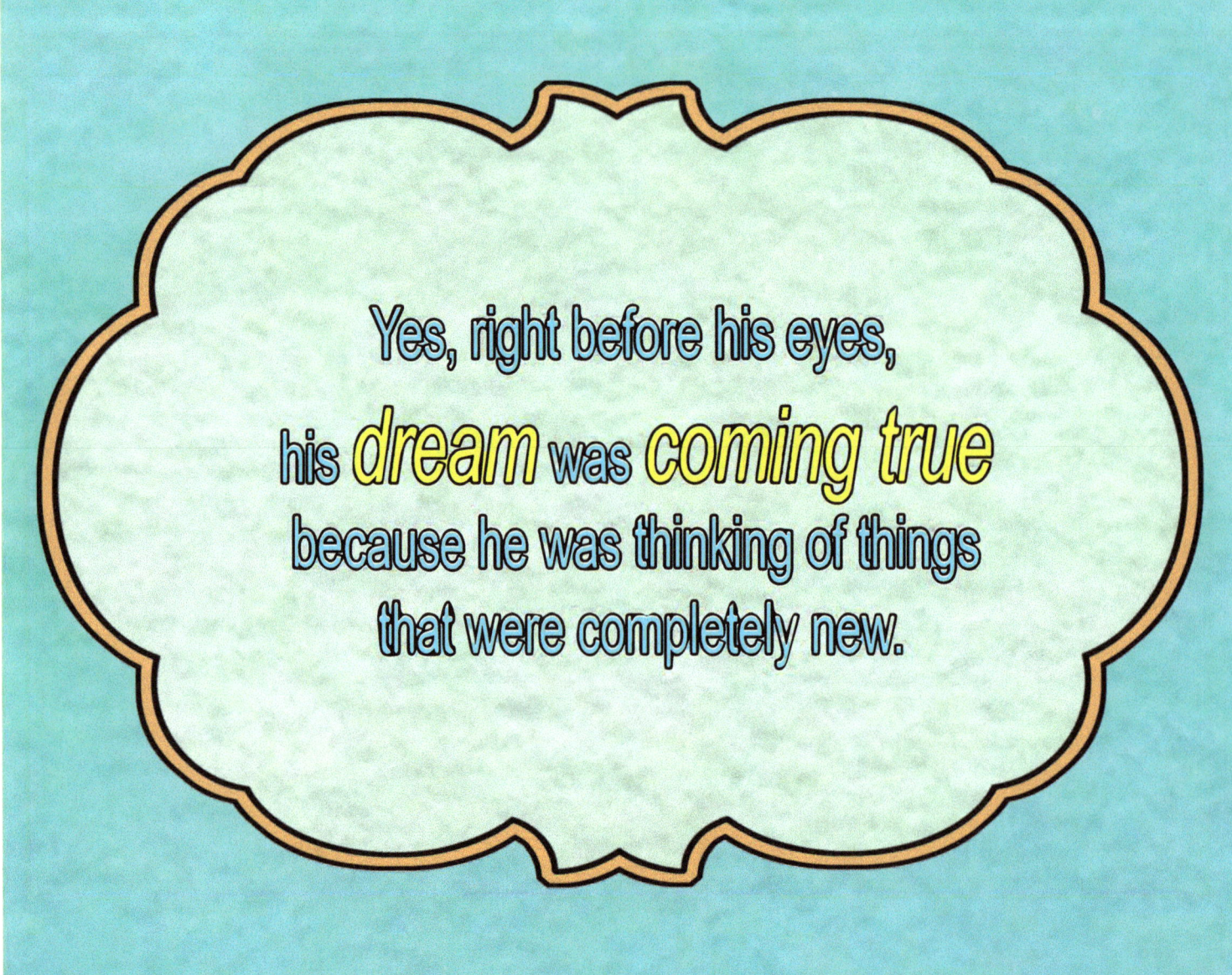

And then, there it was - his machine - ready for flight.
So he took it into the sky ... and it *soared* like a kite!

He flew high into the clouds and towards the sun, and he wasn't just dreaming. He was *really having fun!*

He had done what everyone else said no one could do.
Because he worked long and hard ...
his *dream* had come true!

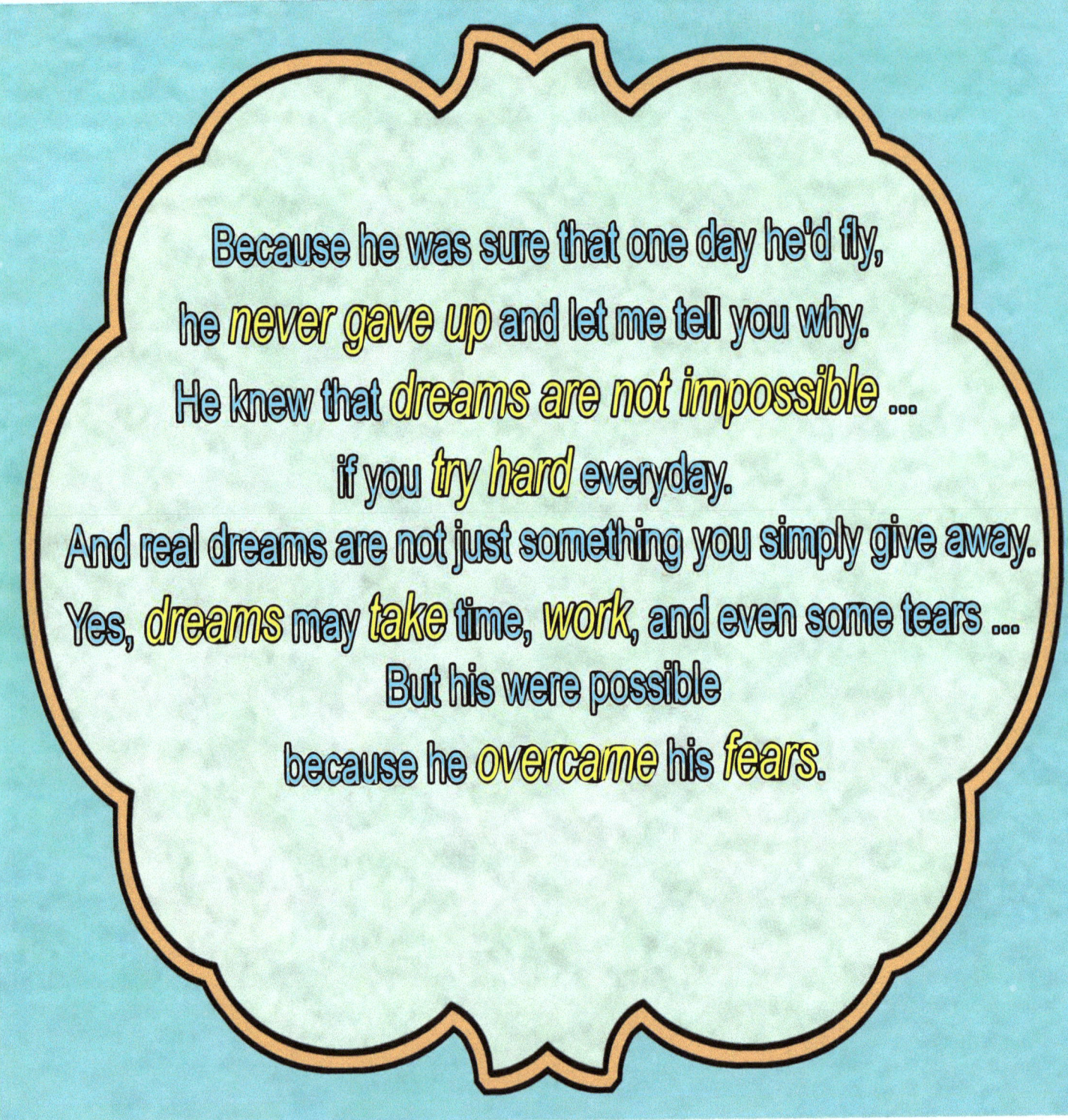

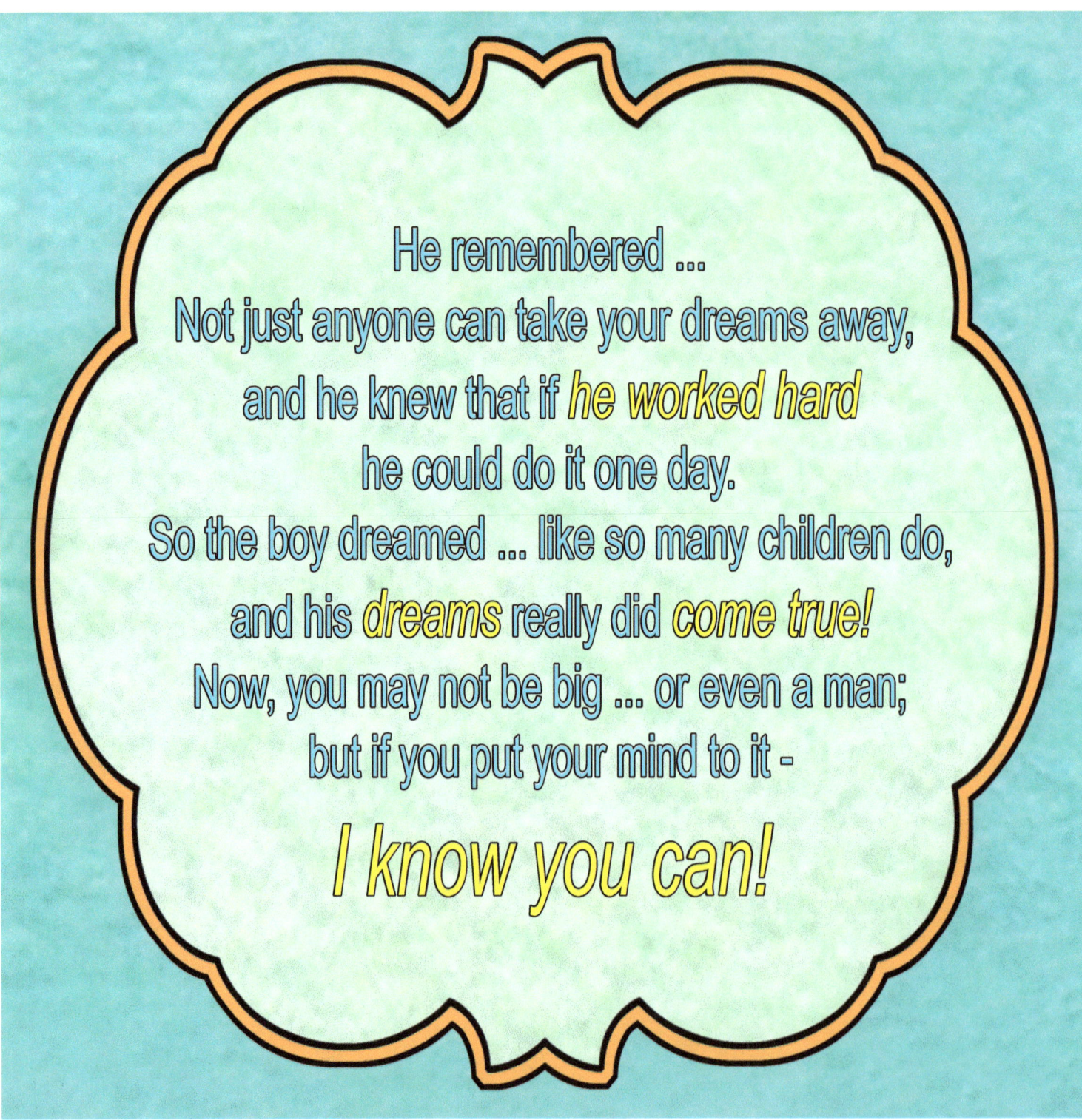

He remembered ...
Not just anyone can take your dreams away,
and he knew that if *he worked hard*
he could do it one day.
So the boy dreamed ... like so many children do,
and his *dreams* really did *come true!*
Now, you may not be big ... or even a man;
but if you put your mind to it -

I know you can!

Sweet dreams...
Goodnight

For more adventures visit us at www.poetrypete.com